I Like to Collect

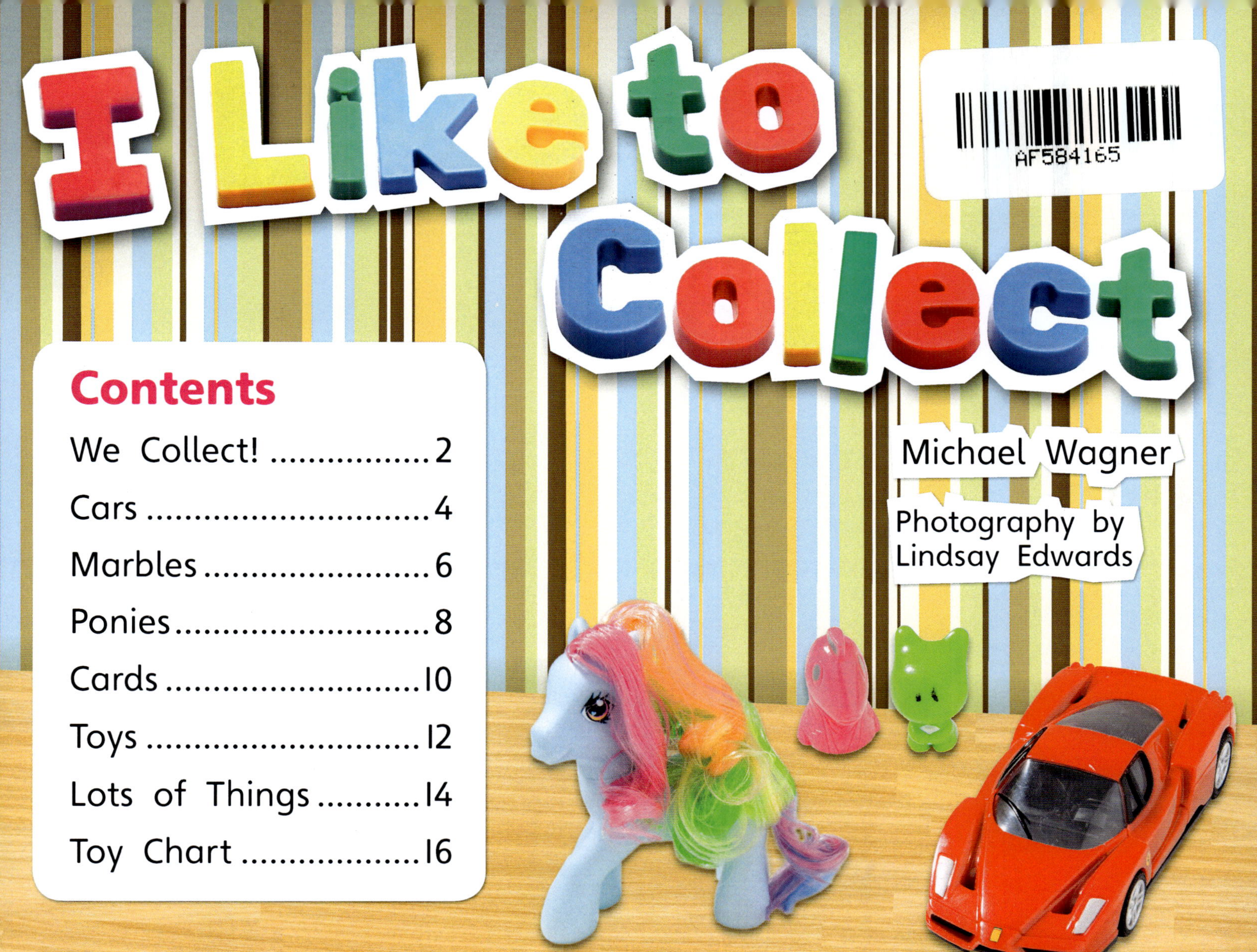

Michael Wagner

Photography by
Lindsay Edwards

Contents

We Collect!

Look at all these things.
We like to collect them.

It is fun to collect things!

Cars

Hi! My name is Tayleb. I collect cars.

I have fast cars.
I have old cars!
These cars are made of metal.

Marbles

Hi! My name is Gary.
I collect marbles.

I have little marbles.
I have big marbles.

Ponies

My name is Alisha.
I collect ponies.

I have blue ponies.
I have pink ponies.
I love ponies.

Cards

My name is Marcelle.
I collect cards.

I swap cards with my friend.
Then I get cards that I like!

Toys

My name is Aidan.
I collect these toys.

I play with my friend.
We put the toys in a line.
We make the toys crash.
It is lots of fun!
These toys are made of plastic.

Lots of Things

There are lots of things to collect.
What do you like best?

Toy Chart
made of glass
made of metal
made of paper
made of plastic
made of plastic
Pokémon